Alaska
WILDLIFE

A Celebration of
WILD and FREE

By Sea • By Land • By Air

By Ron Sanford

Developed and produced by

John Hinde Curteich Inc.

Westlake Village, California 91362

Distributed by J & H Sales

Anchorage, Alaska 99501

Designed by Jerri Hemsworth

Printed in U.S.A.

10 9 8 7 6 5 4 3 2 1

Library of Congress Cataloging-in-Publication Data Pending

Sanford, Ron

Alaska Wildlife: A Celebration of Wild and Free/Ron Sanford

p. cm.

ISBN 1-889467-15-4

1. Alaska Wildlife — North America. 2. Alaska — North America. 3. Wildlife — North America.

4. Wildlife — North America — Pictorial works.   5. Alaska — North America — Pictorial works.

I. Sanford, Ron   II. Title

Whilst every care is taken in compiling this book,

no responsibility can be taken for errors or omissions.

Cover: Bull moose feeds in Wonder Lake. Evening light creates reflection of Mt. McKinley. Denali National Park.

Back Cover: Aurora Borealis (Northern Lights). Bull caribou. Denali National Park.

Alaska
WILDLIFE

A Celebration of
WILD and FREE
By Sea • By Land • By Air

Contents

Preface 4
The Wonder of It All... 5

By Sea 8
Humpback Whale ....8 – 12
Red-Necked Phalaropes 12
Gray Whale 13
Killer Whales ....14 – 15
Bull Walrus 16
Round Island...or Beach Blubber Goes Bananas 17
Walrus ....18 – 19
Sea Otter 20
Harbor Seals 21
Pacific White-Sided Dolphin 22
Stellar Sea Lions 23
Sockeye (Red) Salmon 24

By Land 25
Brown Bear 25
Polar Bear 26
Brown Bear 27
Grizzly Bear 28
Alaska's Annual Ambush At Brooks Falls 30
Black Bear 33
Moose ....34 – 35
Gray Wolf 36
Denali 37
Red Fox 39
Mountain Goat and Dall Sheep Ram 40
Red Squirrel, Arctic Ground Squirrel and Hoary Marmot 41
Beaver ....42 – 43
Bull Caribou ....44 – 45

By Air 46
Tundra Swans 46
Ross and Snow Geese 47
Tufted Puffin 48
Horned Puffin 49
Lesser Yellowlegs, Black-Billed Magpie and Black Oyster-Catcher ...50
Glaucous-Winged Gulls and Black-Legged Kittiwake 51
Willow Ptarmigan ....52 – 53
A Celebration of Eagles 54
Bald Eagle ....54 – 58
The Inside Passage...Unpeopled and Wild 59
Glacial Ice ....61 – 62
LeConte Glacier 63
Denali 64

Preface

Alaska somehow belongs to any heart big enough to receive it. Residents, tourists, and international travelers all experience the drop dead vastness at different levels—from the deck of a luxury cruise ship or from approaching the final ascent of Mount McKinley (or "Denali" to anyone who's been there). Early on (1962-1965), I was a resident and then, starting in 1987, I became a regular visitor.

In the last 5 years, I've devoted a great deal of effort to the humpback whales of Frederick Sound and around. Before that it was the bald eagle, and before that it was the grizzly, and before that...well you get the idea. My photography always seems to get better when I stay longer and work harder.

When I was asked to do this book, my first response was to hopefully create emphasis via *visual celebration* rather than education. They gave me the liberty to roam around rather than deal with the nitty gritty details. It's been fun having the freedom to touch on this and then kinda bypass that. At a mellowing age of 57, "picking and choosing" is becoming a surprise luxury in an Information Highway age that seems to be steadfast in the unending pursuit of statistical data and knowledge that is speeding faster and faster down a seemingly endless road.

Yes, the clouds cling like concrete. *Yes,* the white socks fly incessantly in your face and get caught in your eye when you blink...and the June mosquitoes! *Yes,* it is expensive. *Yes,* the wind always blows the rain into your lens (no matter which direction you turn). Robert Service once wrote, "It's the cussedest land that I know." I guess that if it weren't so good it could be that bad, but I don't know anyone who doesn't savor their time spent in Alaska.

I'm in hopes that this small collection of photographs will allow the viewer a journey back in time to a special moment that will help identify an experience unique to your time spent in the northland. The wildlife of Alaska provides the vital link connecting *wild* to *wilderness.* Without the critter, it's just scenery. ➘

The Wonder of It All...

In the early '60s, I did my obligatory military duty stationed in Alaska. For three and a half years, I served on missile sites surrounding the Anchorage area. When I wasn't working, I was constantly drawn into a stunning wilderness environment I had never known before and few people know today. Even now I hesitate to share intimate details of my experiences because words simply don't convey "The Wonder of It All." It was an era of $25 an hour bush pilots. Put an "X" on a map and the conversation would be as follows: "Well I've never landed in there, but let me call Bill. I think he once mentioned a creek bed in that area...." Well maybe Bill had only flown over it, but it would be Ted who actually got his Piper Super Cub down in the gravel of the glacial moraine, etc. The next opportunity away from work would have us circling the area looking for the spot from a description scratched on the back of a discarded envelope. Each of these types of landings were a little bit like landing on the moon—no one knew for sure whether it could even be done. My partner and I would have to fly in one by one because the Cub was a two seater, giant engine, very large soft tires, with a single stick and hardly an instrument aboard. It was by guess and by golly, add a measure of "seat of the pants."

We were in the Wrangells, the Talkeetnas, the Chugach and the Alaska Ranges. Every creature comfort was on our back. We not only didn't have a cellular phone and 911, but we were fully aware that there was NO ROUTE OUT! It seems like only yesterday, hearing the pilot's voice over the roar of the plane, "I'll check on you in about a week." That meant he would if he could, depending on the weather. We were alone.

After my tour of duty, I returned to my home in California. I was in my mid-twenties and eager to tell a few tales. My first get-together with old chums had me into my first story when I was interrupted by somebody saying, "Yea, I know what you mean, we were camping last weekend around Lake Tahoe." At that point I realized I couldn't tell anyone about "The Wilderness" I had experienced. I shut up then, and remain that way today. I now have a grandson, and maybe in a couple of years, I'll give him a go.

I think my inability with words had something to do with my becoming a photographer. I suspect the images in my head are less descriptive, and more visual. In 1970, I traveled to Japan on business. A dollar could buy 360 yen, and everyone felt obligated to buy both a wrist watch and a camera. I'll spare you the details, but the camera became a WOW in my life to such an extent that it would become my life in a few years.

As a professional photographer, I avoided the unresolved issue of my untold experiences in Alaska for nearly 10 years. In 1987 (22 years later) I sought to put my sense of the magic on film. To my surprise, I found more than I could have imagined. Much of my early wilderness experience centered around survival and adventure. This return marked the beginning of a beginning that has led me down a very different path which allowed me to wonder as I wander. I now can find natural history miracles in my back yard, but it was the second coming of *wild* (Alaska style) that humbled my dominant human instincts. Once I was personally drawn into the "Web of Life" idea I became part of it, and, more importantly, one with it. A spiritual kinship toward subject is more important than camera, lens and film.

The first half of my life is a story of effort and reward. Failure always had something to do with lack of appropriate effort. Football, a girlfriend, a university degree, a job, a house, a life, all seemed to come about if one took charge of the situation—*make it happen.* This worked adequately well in my commercial (Architectural/Corporate) work. It worked less well when I attempted to portray a subject close to my heart. I couldn't make "my" Alaska happen on film. The great gifts of the North (and everywhere you travel for that matter) are only available if you *allow* them to come into your life. To receive without effort requires a little unlearning and a lot of practice. Regrets for yesterday, and an anxiety for tomorrow, seem to rob us of the moment. We seem to find ourselves in a crazy cycle of tending to the elusive somewhere, the someplace and the someone that remains just around the next corner or just above the next step. In my life, and in my work, I've learned that the good stuff happens *here*, and it happens *now.* Some other time always remains some other time.

As I write, I suspect that I have now returned to Alaska at least 15 times since my 1987 trip. I've truly seen and experienced "The Wonder of It All." The photographic process leaves a lot to be desired when scenic splendor and heart stopping action meet in a single frame. I'm currently trying to more closely authenticate field experience and the photographic process via the computer, but none of the photographs in this book are digital (yet).

"Biodiversity" and "sustainability" have become the key words for the decision makers of the future. I can't conclude this segment without expressing my fear for the future of *wild*. I agree that greed and narrow self interest are part of our nature (maybe for a good cause?) but it is in our best interest to make life livable on the only planet we have handy. "Save The Earth" slogans tend to distance us from the problem. The future of us as people is at stake here—the Earth is doing fine, thank you. Give or take a few years, and a few people, I believe it took all of eternity for the people population to reach a billion in 1800. 130 years later (1930) we doubled to two billion, and then four billion by 1960, etc. We have just under 6 billion today and demographics indicate a doubling of that number in less than 50 years. I can't imagine it.

I can't imagine not having a wild place in which to catch my over-civilized breath. I can't imagine not waking up to the sound of geese in the fall. I don't want to imagine that my grandson might travel to an Alaska without wild critters roaming free. I'll never be able to tell him; I'll never be able to show him...how special it *was*. I can't hope to change anyone's mind. The best I can ever hope to do is change me. I work at it nearly every day.

• By Sea •

Breach.

9

Humpback Whale

(Megaptera novaeangliae)

Humpbacks lunge feed for herring in explosive accord.

Blow from a humpback.

Humpback's fluke.

11

Humpback tail lob.

The blow of a humpback along with a flock of Red-Necked Phalaropes.

(Phalaraopus lobatus).

12

13

Gray Whale

(*Eschrichtius robustus*)

Killer Whales

(Orcinus orca)

A killer whale breaches.

Killer whale pod.

15

16

Bull Walrus

(Odobenus rosmarus)

Round Island ...
or Beach Blubber Goes Bananas

There's a place I know where what *was*, still *is*. Alaska's Round Island, in the South Bering Sea, is such a place. Few areas on Earth remain as wild, remote, pristine, teaming with wildlife, and still open to the likes of me and you. If that sounds good to you then maybe I ought to add that the island is also very steep (and most times slippery), rugged, and "by nature" inhospitable to those seeking minimal creature comforts. Nasty weather can set in for weeks, and your tent must be capable of withstanding gale force winds to 60 miles per hour.

Round Island is one of seven craggy, fog wrapped knolls that make up the Walrus Island group in Bristol Bay. A commercial scheduled jet airline will deliver you to Dillingham. Air taxi service is now required to the small native village of Togiak. Next comes Don Winkleman's butt busting boat ride to the island itself.

I was drawn to this location in an effort to add photographic coverage of the Pacific Walrus to my files. Historically, thousands upon thousands of bull walrus haul out onto the beaches of Round Island in midsummer. I can now confirm this to be true, and the spectacle is hard to exaggerate. A friend called this place a *"Walrus Fat Farm."* I find this description to be pretty accurate—what a visual delight. If you can imagine, just the four of us, on a tiny, treeless island (less than two square miles), surrounded by beaches crammed with noisy walrus. To this picture add shear cliffs alive with a million nesting birds, a veritable sea of wildflowers, and toss in a cavorting red fox playing fearlessly at your feet.

Back to getting there, and after our boat ride, we were met by two resident Alaska fish and game biologists. Getting ashore is no simple task. They provided a most tender Tender service, shuttling us from Winkleman's boat to the rocky beach. Then it's up the cliff via foot-holds here and a jutting rock there, aided by a dangling rope to hang on to...or from. Coming and going will be the only time we will be allowed on the beach. This is a walrus sanctuary, and when you apply for an access permit, you will be made accutely aware of your "visitor/guest" status. You're up and the critters are down, but the magic of the place surrounds you. You don't have to unzip the fly on your tent to hear a chorus of snorting, sneezing and snoring. Tune your ears a bit and you'll also audibilize into a "twilight zone" of whistle and bell-like gonging sounds. I can't imagine what these bachelor bulls have on their minds, but when you first hear these strange sounds, it will sit you upright in your sleeping bag. Then blend the wave after wave of strafing kittiwakes shrieking their names, over a pitter patter of precipitation, and you have a cacophony of sound.

This obvious expression of enthusiasm should not be construed as a recommendation for anyone's adventure travel. It's simply not an easy place. In a way, I suppose the hardships involved could be construed as positive force. I understand that only 200 people a year (worldwide) will scramble up the cliffs of "Boat Cove." I want to report that for now, Round Island still *is*, and I hope (somehow) it will always continue to be.

Ａ walrus "Fat Farm"...the spectacle is hard to exaggerate.

20

Sea Otter

(Enhydra lutris)

21

Harbor Seals

(Phora vitulina)

Pacific White-Sided Dolphin

(Lagenorhynchus obliquidens)

Stellar Sea Lion

(Eumetopias jubatus)

A tangled fishing net
and a bleak future...

24

Sockeye (Red) Salmon

(Oncorhynchus nerka)

· By Land ·

Polar Bear

(Ursus maritimus)

Brown Bear

(Ursus arctos)

Sticking one's nose in another's business can have
serious consequences (porcupine quills).

28

Grizzly Bear

(Ursus arctos)

The grizzly and brown bear are one and the same species—
Ursus arctos. If the bear is coastal, we call it a brown bear.
If the bear is interior, we call it a grizzly.

Alaska's Annual Ambush
At Brooks Falls

A vintage twin engine "Goose" banks above Naknek Lake, and Brooks Lodge comes into view. We are about to experience Katmai National Park, and if you don't get wet getting from the float plane to the beach, you undoubtedly will before you make camp some half mile away. It's not required that one look up to make a weather assessment—it's either raining, has just quit, or is about to begin. This happens to be an area where major weather systems from the Gulf of Alaska and Siberia bump heads.

This land of Katmai received world attention in 1912 when a cataclysmic volcanic eruption (10 times more forceful than the 1980 eruption of Mount Saint Helens) created a geothermal phenomenon that was (and is today) labeled the Valley of 10,000 Smokes. For several days the ash, pumice, and gas darkened the skies over most of the Northern Hemisphere.

However, the eruption we were anxiously anticipating occurs here yearly as the sockeye (red) salmon come rushing home after maturing for several years in the North Pacific. In July, the return of spawning salmon is as predictable as the arrival of the massive brown bears who gather to greet them. We were about to witness and record a rare and endangered wildlife opportunity. Here all the forces of nature focus on the world's largest carnivore—the Alaskan "brownie."

Philosophically, the Park Service has done a magnificent job. The rangers see their job as managing people, not bears. Visitors are transient guests. The bears are at home, and they literally have no other place left on Earth to go. A "bad" bear must be destroyed, but even the very idea of bad or good is almost always directly related to how man has previously "conditioned" the circumstance. During the salmon migration, bear are single-minded and gluttonously busy, but they are also opportunists. Create an opportunity and you create a problem. Bears seem to function by doing that which derives for them a direct benefit. The delicate balance of man and beast seems to thrive at Katmai because every visitor, even before they exit the beach on landing, is instructed on how *not* to benefit bear.

Our photographic study of "fishing" brown bear began without a camera, at Brooks Falls (a perfect viewing location approximately 2 miles by trail from camp). To get ahead of the action, one attempts first to understand it. It takes a lot of looking and learning. More than 2 dozen bear will frequent this area during the summer. We first observed that most salmon, successfully clearing the top of the cascading water, made their wild leap from a well defined area along the falls. Secondly, we began to ID separate animals, and were able to determine that each bear not only had a favorite spot, but also a unique fishing style. Finally, we could sense a hierarchy in the ranks, and the presence of the more dominant members bore heavily on the activity of the others. Each new understanding became a wonderful revelation in the nature of this most natural world. From this information base, our approach to the actual photography remained pretty much the same as other work we do with wildlife. The idea is to study, understand, predict and visually intercept at a peak of "gesture," but not interfere.

In conclusion, I must say that if you are, indeed, fortunate enough to visit this remarkable wilderness, it will matter little what your goal is (fishing, hiking, camping or just staying at the lodge), or who you are (photographer, naturalist or volcanist), *you will come away with your very own bear story.* I'll spare you ours!

Bear Facts

The brown bears of Alaska are the largest land predators in North America, nearly twice as large as their inland cousin, the Alaska grizzly. (Alaska's brown bears and grizzlies are now considered one species, *Ursus arctos.*) A protein-rich diet of salmon, during the summer spawning season, is thought to contribute to the massive size attained by the coastal cousin. When the supply of salmon exhausts itself, the bears retreat to higher elevations and concentrate their dietary efforts on the summer's bounty of wild berries. Well fortified by fishing and foraging, the big browns dig a fresh den to which they will retire sometime in November. Here they hibernate through the cold, dark months of winter. A bear's hibernation alternates between periods of slumber and wakefulness, during which the bear may even emerge from its den for a short period of time. Mated sows give birth during hibernation. The newborn cub(s) rarely weigh much more than a pound each. They are nearly helpless at birth, but grow rapidly. When the new family emerges from the den in April, they must be capable of traveling together. Cubs remain with their mother for two years during which time she will protect, feed, teach and discipline them in the ways of the wilderness.

Following the 5 to 6 months of denning, brown bears wake in the spring to mate, to socialize and to feed. The bears' appetites are voracious and they feed almost continuously. Vegetation is the mainstay of their diet until the salmon run starts in June or July. Brown bears tend to congregate where there is a source of food and social interaction begins. In Katmai National Park, the bears concentrate their fishing efforts at Brooks Falls where the salmon pause before hurling themselves at this formidable barrier. Bears continually struggle for social position and dominance, developing a social hierarchy on the river. The largest, strongest males secure the best fishing sites, next come other high ranking males, then sows with cubs, sows without cubs, sibling groups and lastly small loners. When satiated, a brown will consume only the gourmet (by bear standards) portions of a salmon (usually the bellies, brains and egg sacks) casting off nearly whole fish to float down stream. Less successful fishing bears, and an entourage of gulls, eagerly consume these leftovers. On the Brooks River, we observed a wide variety of very patented fishing styles. Some individuals demonstrated great skill, savvy, technique and success. Others appeared inept and mostly ineffective. They also seemed unwilling to observe and modify. One dominant male, whom we had dubbed "scar face," positioned himself at the base of the falls and methodically caught and consumed 10 salmon in a matter of minutes. A young adult brown thrashed wildly about, in his fishing attempt, only to come up empty handed. And yet another young adult chose to position himself at the top of the falls where he patiently, and expertly, caught one salmon after another in mid-flight.

The brown bears of Alaska are intelligent. They have a predator's instinct for survival which contributes to their unnerving reputation of being a bit unpredictable. At Katmai, bears do have the right of way. A person should "instinctively" discover that backpedaling is a good idea if a brown bear (some weighing up to 900 lbs.) is coming down the same trail you're going up. However, one should *never run*. Such action would undoubtedly trigger the bear's natural instinct to chase and any single bear can move twice as fast as any single human. Two other things to keep in mind are *avoid surprise*—make noise as you hike; and *never do anything that even begins to threaten a cub*—real or otherwise.

Visitors who are mindful and respectful of the Alaskan brown bear have, even today, a rare and wonderful opportunity to observe this magnificent animal in a natural state. The park people at Katmai continue to demonstrate a policy of effective wildlife management. Simply stated, the bears are allowed to do what bears do—people must conform accordingly.

Black Bear

(Ursus americanus)

33

Cow and twin calves feed in Wonder Lake below Mt. McKinley.

34

Moose

(Alces alces)

Bull Moose.

Gray Wolf

(Canis lupus)

Denali

Alaska's Denali National Park is less a place and more a state of mind—less a national park and more an international treasure. This is the last of what was and can never be again. It is a vast (6 million acres) wilderness, and a continuing habitat larger than the state of Massachusetts. At well over 20,000 feet, Mount McKinley is the *largest* mountain on Earth when one considers that it consistently towers some 3 miles higher than its surrounding area. Unfortunately, many visitors must buy the post cards for a peek at the peak. The mountain literally creates its own weather systems, and summer cloud patterns obscure the view looking up 70% of the time.

Private vehicles are not permitted in the park beyond the Savage River Bridge at the 12-mile mark. To fully access the 85-mile road to Wonder Lake, visitors must tour by bus. If you're headed for the end of the road, plan on a very full 10-hour day of going in and coming out.

In 1917, the park was originally established to protect its large mammals, and these critters today still highlight one's visit. The buses make scheduled stops along the route, but the unscheduled stops are at the heart of the drive. The driver will never knowingly pass without stopping at the sighting of a grizzly bear, dall sheep, caribou, gray wolf, moose, fox, beaver or golden eagle. The list continues, but what you might realistically expect to see on your one day in the park can range from disappointing to nothing short of mind blowing. There's no better place on earth to *experience* northern wildlife. The animals seemingly have grown to ignore, or at least tolerate the vehicles on the road, and people in general. At Eielson Visitor Center, I was having a sandwich among a crowd of tourists coming and going, loading and unloading, as a result of a backup of busses converging in a narrow frame of time. In mid-summer this is always a busy spot, but at this moment "chaos" would be a fair description of the human activity. In this setting, a couple of very large bull caribou had selected the gravel and shade of the visitor center to escape the pesky insects and take a nap. Rangers were holding the picture takers a safe distance away when a grizzly sow and cubs strolled into the picture. Of course then it became a herding task for the staff to quickly assemble everyone onto the viewing platform. Cameras were ready as the bear family approached, but in the interim, a red fox began a life and death chase—zigging and zagging just behind an Arctic ground squirrel. All eyes were now focused straight down as the mother bear also witnessed the kill. The fox, now aware of three grizzlies racing to the crime site, decided the best thing to do was to bury the body. The story continues, but I won't, other than to add that this small tale describes the unpredictability of what one might see in this special place on any given day.

That's the good news. The bad news is that Denali National Park is no secret. My first intro came in 1963, at a time when 15,000 visitors could be expected in a summer. Today that number has increased to more than 600,000, and there's still one road in and out. It's a short season—June, July and August (with maybe a week or two on either side). Whether you plan a do-it-on-your-own or whether you want/need a fully escorted tour, the best plan is to have a plan. You might start by requesting information from: The Superintendent, Denali National Park, P.O. Box 9, Denali National Park, Alaska 99755. It's WILD...

Gray Wolf.

Red Fox

(Vulpes vulpes)

39

Mountain Goat Nanny

(Oreamnos americanus)

Dall Sheep Ram

(Ovis dalli)

Red Squirrel

(Tamiasciurus hudsonicus)

Arctic Ground Squirrel

(Spermophilus parryii)

41

Hoary Marmot

(Marmota caligata)

Beaver

(Castor canadensis)

Nature's second greatest landscape architect.

Bull Caribou

(Rangifer tarandus)

· By Air ·

Snow and Ross' Geese

(Chen caerulescens, Chen rossii)

48

Tufted Puffin

(Fratercula cirrhata)

49

Horned Puffin

(Fratercula corniculata)

Lesser Yellowlegs

(Tringa flavipes)

Black-Billed Magpie

(Pica pica)

Black Oyster-Catcher

(Haematopus bachmani)

Glaucous-Winged Gulls

(Larus glaucescens)

Black-Legged Kittiwake

(Rissa brevirostris)

Willow Ptarmigan

(Lagopus lagopus)

Plummage to winter white.

A Celebration of Eagles

Few people can resist stopping to stare at the sight of a bald eagle soaring overhead. With a wing span of up to 8 feet and the capacity of attaining speeds approaching 100 mph, a bald eagle in flight is a majestic sight. Courtship displays in early April are a real heart stopper. With talons locked, the couple somersaults and dives through the air in powerful swoops to consummate the act of bonding. Summer visitors to southeast Alaska's panhandle (Ketchikan to Haines) have an excellent opportunity to experience both the abundance of wildlife and a spectacular glaciated rain forest—truly the land of the eagle. Both bird and marine mammal are drawn to the waters of Frederick Sound by the abundant schools of herring churning at the surface.

In the late fall and early winter, near Haines, one can expect to see the largest gathering of eagles anywhere on Earth. Along a 5-mile stretch of the Chilkat River, a late run of spawning chum salmon seek the warm water upwellings which keep the river free of ice. This unique food source attracts more than 3,000 bald eagles from all over Alaska, British Columbia and as far away as the state of Washington.

By the early 1950's, nearly 130,000 eagles had already been shot for bounty, but when Alaska became a state, the bald eagle came under federal protection. In 1972, the "Valley of the Eagle," along the Chilkat River, was recognized as critical habitat, and in 1982, some 48,000 acres were finally set aside as the Alaska Chilkat Bald Eagle Preserve.

If you want to celebrate, first hand, with the Eagles and need more information about specific visitor services, write to the Chamber of Commerce, P.O. Box 518, Haines, Alaska 99827, or to Alaska State Parks, Department of Natural Resources, Division of Parks and Recreation, 400 Willoughby, Juneau, Alaska 99801.

55

Bald Eagle

(Haliaeetus leucocephalus)

The Inside Passage...
Unpeopled and Wild

How many people know southeast Alaska's panhandle as the "Alexander Archipelago?" Most (and that's becoming a bunch!) know this area as the summer "Inside Passage" route for cruise ships, stopping at places named Ketchikan, Sitka, Juneau, etc., on a voyage heading for a visual climax in Glacier Bay. Many also travel these waters on the so-called "Blue Canoes" of the Alaska Marine Highway. One can also arrive by air, but you won't/can't arrive by car. This is a land of rugged isolation, separated from the outside world by snow-capped rocks towering over massive ice fields. Glaciers abound.

Clinging to the water's edge (some 11,000 miles of it) is a land reborn from the last ice age and bursting with life. It is believed that man crossed the Bering Land Bridge 40,000 years ago and moved south. The Tlingit Indians (and other natives) have a rich history of mastering navigation and canoe building. The totem parks of Ketchikan are a delightful way to invest quality time. Early white settlers were a colorful "Boom & Bust" bunch for which many tales are told. In the early part of this century, the poet Robert Service found just the right words to insure that this bit of our history will live on forever.

But my interest is less into the people and more into the natural history. The passengers aboard the ferries and cruise ships love it, but they can only guess what's in the cove, or up the fiord, or on the island (and there are literally thousands of them). Ninety percent of the panhandle belongs to you. The Tongass National Forest is the largest in the nation. I hate statistics, but 17,000,000 acres is a lot of habitat, and with some place to roam, wild critters abound. Wildlife that is "threatened," or even "endangered" elsewhere, is abundant here. The bald eagle and brown bear are classic examples.

As a wildlife photographer, there are many major obstacles in a process that attempts to tell a story of light, gesture and stage on a frozen frame of film. Three challenges loom high above the rest—*location, timing* and *approachability;* southeast Alaska is a simply wonderful area for "watchable" wildlife.

In my younger years, I used a variety of light power boats to get around. One can increase the chances for truly magic moments when you have that kind of flexibility and freedom. We would camp on the beaches, and then roam the back waters. Hiking is most times limited to where we could penetrate the dense temperate rain forest, along animal trails, or along stream beds. The other side of this type of venture is weather, major tidal "ups and downs" and opportunistic free roaming bear. As I sit here in California, I can predict *your* weather, on *your* southeast Alaska expedition, whenever *you* decide to go—"A chance of rain." Just outside the Inside Passage lies the Gulf of Alaska. How many times have you heard the weatherman describe a storm coming out of *the Gulf of Alaska?* I've crossed what I consider a narrow body of "flat" water only to have the wind begin to blow and we'd start taking waves over the side within minutes. Tides are another matter, but can be just as frightening. When large bodies of water are separated by a narrow or shallow passage, it has the makings of big trouble for small boats (and big boats, too). There's also the annoying factor of anchoring your boat. We would use plastic bottles, ropes and pulleys, etc. The process is not complicated, but it's time consuming. Finally our beach patrolling bruin friends never seem to get it straight as to what food is theirs and what food is ours...and they can be big bullies about it. Worse than that, when thoughtless campers make foolish food storage mistakes, it creates a "bad?" bear. Bad bear can be a danger to other unsuspecting people, and they are then either relocated or *shot.* While on the subject of bear, I should mention at least two wonderful places to photograph bear during the salmon runs: Pack Creek on Admiralty Island (a short plane flight out of Juneau (which is good for brown bear) and Anan Creek (the best place I know to enjoy the antics of a variety of fishing black bear). I might also add that the Forest Service offers a cabin at Anan and more than 140 at other remote locations in the Tongass.

Tidewater glaciers offer boaters an exciting opportunity to explore the world of ice. Endicott Arm and Tracy Arm, off of Stephens Passage, are wonderful day trips out of Juneau. LeConte Glacier, out of Petersburg, has the most sensational bay of icebergs that I've personally experienced. In July, the harbor seals are pupping on the ice, away from transient pods of killer whales. I understand that the chaos and noise of the calving glacier discourages the orcas from entering the bay.

Petersburg is a very small fishing village away from the influence of cruise ship activity. The Sons of Norway Hall offers a clue as to its Scandinavian heritage. I know the community well because this is where I board the *Delphinus* when I'm working the waters of Frederick Sound. I was tempted to title this piece "Fred. Sound and Around" for this is the area I keep returning to. This body of water attracts the largest concentration of feeding humpback whales in the world. Summer after summer, I've personally witnessed (over and over again) up to 15 gentle giants creating bubble-net circles of confusion around large schools of herring, and then in a well organized explosive lunge, mouths agape, they'd come roaring into aerial feeding displays. Place a few bald eagles just above the action and it gets pretty exciting. Last summer, we had four separate feeding groups (maybe 30 or so whales in total) working an area of Chatham Straight, and then add (in the middle of this activity) a killer whale attack on a couple Dall porpoises. We had a hydra phone aboard so as to eavesdrop on the humpbacks during their strategy session. I find their songs hauntingly beautiful as I try to contemplate the innovation, planning and leadership skills required among the participants. Forty tons per predator versus 4 ounces per prey is problematic when that 4 ounces can add up to a ton of fish consumed in a single day. As an added surprise, and in the spirit of pure joy (at least from my perspective) a whale can breach nearly clear out of the water, followed by a wet explosion at reentry. This burst of unexplained energy can continue dozens of times, and other animals might join in.

Any day in Frederick Sound has an unrehearsed one-of-a-kind quality about it. Rarely have I seen what I consider a repeat performance. Killer whales always arrive unannounced, and whatever we are doing comes to a stop. They always dominate everyone's attention. Rarely does the boat not run across a large rookery of endangered Stellar sea lions. They seem to crave closeness, but then endlessly complain about overcrowding. Watch awhile and you will witness a strange blend of comedy and tragedy (see bottom photo of page 23).

When we drop anchor for the evening in such places as Portage Bay, Windfall Harbor or Snug Cove, and when the day quietly and beautifully comes to an end, Robert Service's "...plumb full of hush" takes on a special meaning. The late afternoon mist hangs low on a *wild* that seems, at least for the moment, to have no end. ↗

This chunk of ice, approximately 10 stories high, broke off the face of LeConte Glacier. This sequence of photos was made while in "rapid retreat."

There is only one Denali.